Skills for Resolving Conflict

Handling Stress

by

Marna Owen

GLOBE FEARON EDUCATIONAL PUBLISHER
A Division of Simon & Schuster
Upper Saddle River, New Jersey

Project Editors: Helene Avraham, Laura Baselice, Lynn W. Kloss
Executive Editor: Joan Carrafiello
Production Manager: Penny Gibson
Production Editor: Nicole Cypher
Marketing Manager: Marjorie Curson
Interior Electronic Design: Patricia Smythe
Illustrator: Donna Nettis
Photo Research: Jenifer Hixson
Electronic Page Production: Eric Dawson
Cover Design: Eric Dawson
Cover Photograph: © Steve and Mary Beran Skjold

Reviewers:

Dorie L. Knaub, B.A., M.S.
Special Education Specialist
Downey Unified School District
Downey, California

Odalis Veronica Martin, B.A., M.S.
Special Education Teacher
Dade County Public Schools
Miami, Florida

Photo Credits: **p. 12:** © Radi Nabulsi; **p. 24:** Steve and Mary Beran Skjold; **p. 26:** © Radi Nabulsi; **p. 36:** © Radi Nabulsi; **p. 46:** Barbara Rios/Photo Researchers; **p. 47:** J. Sloane/The Picture Cube; **p. 60:** David R. Frazier/Photo Researchers

Printed in the United States of America. 1 2 3 4 5 6 7 8 9 10 99 98 97 96 95

ISBN: 0-8359-1273-6

GLOBE FEARON EDUCATIONAL PUBLISHER
A Division of Simon & Schuster
Upper Saddle River, New Jersey

Contents

Chapter 1

Handling Stress

Chapter Objectives

- Describe stress.
- Explain how the body reacts to stress.
- Explain when stress is harmful.

Words to Know

stress: the body's reaction to a new or changing situation

environment (in-VY-run-munt): physical and social surroundings

exhaustion (ig-ZAWS-chun): state of extreme tiredness

What is Wrong?

Rhonda, a fifteen-year-old girl, looked up at her new school. She didn't like what she saw. The school looked cold and unfriendly. Some kids rushed past her. Others gathered in small clusters, talking and laughing. Nobody looked at her.

Rhonda had just been through two tough years. Her father had started to drink too much. He rarely came home. When he did, her parents would argue.

After many bitter words, Rhonda's parents divorced. Rhonda and her mother moved to another town. Their new apartment was quiet. Things seemed to be getting better.

But the sight of this new school was too much for Rhonda. She stood facing it, unable to move.

"What's wrong with me?" Rhonda thought to herself. "By this time, I should be able to face anything. But I just can't go into that school. I can't deal with it."

Where Stress Comes From

Rhonda is experiencing stress. **Stress** is the body's reaction to any new or changing situation. Stress occurs when you view a new situation as a threat or danger. There are three main sources of stress. They are:

- your **environment** (in-VY-run-munt), or your physical and social surroundings
- physical changes in the body
- your thoughts

Your Environment

Do you find your present environment stressful?

Your environment includes buildings, people, sounds, and temperature. Some environments are peaceful and organized. Others are noisy and confusing. As a rule, the more change there is in an environment, the more stressful it is.

Rhonda experienced stress at home when her parents fought. She also experienced stress when she moved away, even though this was a positive change.

> ## ➤ Think About It

Identify an environment that you find stressful.

_____

Your Body

Physical changes in your body are another source of stress. Teenagers are under more stress than many people. During this stage in your life, your body is growing and changing at a fast rate. Even though these changes are quite normal, they do cause stress. Other sources of stress include sickness, poor eating habits, lack of sleep, pregnancy, and disease.

Your Thoughts

Perhaps the most important source of stress is your thoughts. The way you see things and judge them greatly determines the amount of stress you feel. Think about Rhonda. She saw her school as a harsh, unfriendly place. This caused her stress. What might have happened if she had viewed the school as part of a more peaceful life? What if Rhonda had looked at the school as a step toward an easier life at home? She probably wouldn't have felt the same degree of stress. By changing her thoughts, Rhonda could control her stress.

➤ **Stress Builder**

Read each story below. Identify the cause of stress for each person. In some cases, there may be more than one cause.

1. Jerome lives in a tough neighborhood. Some nights, he hears gunshots. Usually, he cannot get to sleep after he hears shots. He's often afraid.

_____

_____

2. Liza wants to attend a certain college. On the day she is to take a college entrance exam, Liza tells her friend, "I know I'm going to fail."

_____

_____

Fight or Flight

As Rhonda stood frozen in front of the school, a group of kids walked up to her. "What's wrong with you?" one girl asked. "Are you sick or something?"

Rhonda's heart began to beat. She felt her blood pumping. Part of her wanted to run. Another part of her wanted to fight. She didn't know what to do.

Have you ever felt the urge to flee a stressful situation?

Rhonda was feeling how her body was reacting to stress. Scientists have discovered that the human body reacts to stress in three stages. First, the mind tells the body that it senses danger. The body reacts in alarm. It releases chemicals that provide extra strength and help to protect against pain. The body systems begin to work faster. Breathing rate increases. The person sweats, or perspires, more. These changes help the person fight, or run, harder than he or she would under normal conditions.

When the stressful situation stops, the body begins to return to normal. The heart rate slows down and the blood pressure decreases. If the stress continues, the body reaches a state of

exhaustion (ig-ZAWS-chun), or extreme tiredness. It cannot keep up the extra energy levels. Body organs, such as the heart, may become damaged.

If you have ever been in an accident or a fight, you may have felt this stress reaction. Scientists think that the stress reaction dates back to our earliest ancestors. It helped humans to react to danger in nature or with other humans.

Signs of Stress

The stress reaction is one way your body shows it is reacting to stress. There are many other signs of stress. The way you think, and what you feel, are also indicators that you are under stress. Some of these "stress signs" are:

- Tension
- Nervousness
- Depression
- Anger
- Fear
- Backaches
- Muscle aches

- Headaches
- Upset stomach
- Eating too little
- Sleeping too little
- Weakness
- Eating too much
- Sleeping too much

➤ **Stress and You**

Can you think of any other signs of stress? List them below. _____

_____

_____

➤ Stress and You

Think about a past situation when you felt danger or were really scared. Describe
the situation and how you felt. _____

_____

_____

Handling Stress

Rhonda faced the group and took a deep
breath. She told herself, "I have nothing to be
afraid of." Then she told the students, "I'm new
here. I'm not sure where I should report for
class."

One of the girls looked Rhonda over carefully. "Come with us," she said. "We'll show you around."

Rhonda sighed with relief. Maybe things would work out. She felt better already!

Rhonda did a good job of coping, or dealing with her stress. She could have run or gotten into a fight. Instead, she turned a stressful situation into a positive one.

Stress is a part of life. You cannot make it disappear completely, nor would you want to. Stress can give you the energy to face challenges and meet them. Think about a basketball player who has to make a game-winning free throw. Without stress, the player may not have the drive or the energy to succeed.

Any type of change, even a positive one, can cause stress.

Too Much Stress!

Stress is harmful when you have too much of it, or when you don't handle it well. The stress reaction causes great "wear-and-tear" on the human body. Heart disease, suicide, alcohol and other drug abuse, and family violence can result from stress. For these reasons, it is important to learn healthy ways to prevent, reduce, or cope with stress. Working through the rest of this book will give you some ideas of how to handle stress.

➤ **Think About It**

1. Why do you think people need to learn how to handle stress?

Chapter Summary

- Stress is the body's reaction to a new or changing situation. The three main sources of stress are your environment, your body, and your thoughts.
- When the mind senses danger, the body reacts in alarm. It releases chemicals that provide added strength and protect against pain. Signs of stress include tension, fear nervousness, depression, and anger.
- Stress is harmful when you have too much of it, or don't handle it well. Stress can be linked to disease and contributes to suicide, alcohol and drug abuse, and violence.

Chapter Review

Words to Know

Complete each sentence with a term listed below.

environment   exhaustion   stress

1. Headaches and backaches are both signs of _____.

2. The noise around you is part of your _____.

3. Her body was so tired that she was in a state of _____.

About Stress

Answer each question in the space provided.

1. What is stress? _____

_____

2. List five signs of stress. _____

_____

_____

Getting Personal

Describe a time when stress helped you meet a challenge._____

_____

_____

Chapter 2

Relax!

Chapter Objectives

- Identify stressful events.
- Explain the importance of learning to relax.
- Practice three ways to relax.

Words to Know

stressor: event that causes stress

meditation (med-uh-TAY-shun): deep, continued
    thought

Test Tension

When Luis woke up for school, he
immediately felt sick. His head hurt and his
stomach was upset. He told his mother he
didn't think he could make it to school. She
responded by taking his temperature.

"It reads normal," she said. "Go to school. If
you still feel badly by lunch time, call me at
work. I'll come get you."

Luis went to school. He felt jumpy and
nervous. One of his friends noticed that he
wasn't acting like himself. He asked Luis,
"What's wrong?"

"I don't know what it is," Luis replied. "I'm
feeling really tense today."

"Well, you'd better relax," his friend said.
"We have that big test coming up in the next
class. If you don't get a good grade, you'll fail
for the term. You'll end up in summer school.
You won't even be able to play on the summer
baseball team."

Luis felt a light bulb go off in his head. The
test! That was where all the tension was
coming from. Now, if only he could figure out a
way to deal with it!

If you were Luis's friend, what would you advise him to do?

Be Aware of Stressors

Sometimes, stress can help you meet a challenge. Too much stress, however, can prevent you from meeting a goal. This is what is happening to Luis. One way that he could reduce his stress is to relax.

Learning to relax is a skill. You have to learn to relax just like you learn to read, throw a ball, or fix a car. All it takes is information and practice.

The first step in learning to relax is to become aware of **stressors**, or events that usually cause you stress. You may already know some of the stressors in your life. They can be major events, such as moving or taking a midterm exam. They can also be everyday events, such as forgetting to do something. Below is a list of some common stressors.

Stressors

- Death of a loved one
- Parent's divorce
- Moving to a new neighborhood
- Ending or beginning a friendship
- Starting a new job
- Taking a test
- Being late
- Arguing with others
- Being arrested
- Pregnancy

What would you add to this list?

_____

_____

➤ **Stress Diary**

During the next week, write down the times when you feel stress.

1. Write the time of day when you feel stress in the column marked **Time**.

2. Identify the sign that indicated you were under stress in the column marked **Stress Sign**.

3. Record what is happening in your environment during your time of stress in the column marked **Stressful Event**. The first one is done for you.

Personal Stress Diary

Date: _____

Time	Stress Sign	Stressful Event
12:30	tension in my shoulders	noisy lunchroom while I am trying to study

Practice Makes Perfect

When Luis kept a stress diary, he found that he almost always felt sick before a test. He went to his school counselor. "What can I do?" Luis asked. "Should I just stop taking tests?"

His counselor shook her head. "If you did that, you would just be creating another stressful situation. It would be better if you just learned how to relax."

Luis's counselor taught him several ways to relax. Luis practiced relaxing his muscles. He practiced deep breathing. He learned to take his mind off the test. When Luis was familiar with these skills, his counselor gave him some advice.

How do you relax?

"Practice these exercises every day until they become as automatic as brushing your teeth. Whenever you know you have to take a test, be on alert. If you feel yourself getting tense, work on relaxing yourself."

Luis's counselor gave him some good advice. When you are in a stressful situation, your muscles react by becoming tense. Learning to relax your muscles can actually relieve the stress. The following activity will provide you with some important tips on how you can relax!

➤ Muscle Mush

This exercise will help you relax your muscles. Practice it daily.

1. Sit in a chair or lie down in a quiet place.

2. Clench your fists tightly for five seconds. Feel the tension in your hands. Let go of the tension and feel your muscles relax. Stay in this relaxed position for 30 seconds.

3. Repeat the exercise with your elbows and upper arm muscles. Tense your arms for five seconds. Then, relax for 30 seconds. Feel the tension slip away. Think about this feeling.

4. Now focus on your face and head. Wrinkle your forehead. Close your eyes tightly. Clench your teeth. Now release your muscles. Feel your face relax. Let your jaw drop. Take a deep breath. When you exhale, or let the air out, feel the tension drain away.

5. Tense your shoulders and neck. Shrug your shoulders, bringing them toward your ears. Hold for five seconds, then relax. Notice the difference in your neck and shoulder muscles.

6. Repeat the exercise with your stomach, legs, and feet. Each time, remember how your muscles feel tensed, and then relaxed. Breathe deeply each time you relax.

Breathe It In!

Breathing deeply brings oxygen to your muscles and helps you relax. The following exercises will help improve your breathing.

➤ Deep Breathing

1. Stand or sit up straight. Breathe through your nose.

2. Take in a long, deep breath. As you inhale, fill the low section of your lungs first. Your stomach will be pushed down and out to make room for the air.

3. Now, fill the middle part of your lungs with air. You will feel your ribs and chest move out.

4. Finally, take air into the upper part of your lungs. Feel your chest fill out completely. Try not to move your shoulders upward.

5. Hold the breath for several seconds, then release it. Use your stomach muscles to push out the last bit of air.

➤ **Let It All Out**

Use this exercise when you are tired or tense.

1. Stand or sit up straight.

2. Take a deep breath.

3. As you exhale, or let the air move out of your body, let out a long sigh.

4. Breathe in and repeat the exercise ten times.

Empty Your Mind

Another way to relax is through **meditation** (med-uh-TAY-shun), or deep, continued thought. In meditation, you actually try to clear out, or empty, your mind. This may sound easy, but it takes a lot of practice. Here is a good way to begin.

➤ Counting Meditation

1. Find a comfortable position. Meditation works best when you are comfortable.

2. Take a deep breath.

3. As you exhale, say the number "one" to yourself.

4. Continue to breathe in and out. With each breath you let out, say the next number to yourself. Continue in this manner until you reach the number four.

5. Repeat the exercise, beginning with the number one.

Walking Meditation

Repeat the steps involved in counting meditation while taking a walk. Instead of counting breaths, count each time your right foot hits the ground. Count from one to four, then begin again.

➤ Relax Yourself!

Now that you know how to relax, complete this final exercise.

1. Look back at your stress diary. In which of these situations would you like to be more relaxed? Explain why.

_____

_____

_____

2. Imagine yourself in that situation. What will you do to relax?

_____

_____

_____

> ## Use It!

In this section, you learned some different exercises that can help you relax. Practice these exercises every day. Use them whenever you feel yourself becoming stressed out. After you have used the exercises more than once, answer the following questions.

1. Describe a time when you used the exercises to relax.

_____

_____

2. Which exercise did you use?

_____

3. How did your muscles feel after using the exercise?

_____

_____

4. What effect did the exercise have on your thoughts and feelings?

_____

_____

Chapter Summary

- Both major events and common everyday occurrences can cause stress. The first step in controlling stress is being aware of stressors and stress signs.
- When you are under stress, your muscles become tense. Learning to relax is one way to help reduce the stress.
- Learning to relax takes practice. Tensing and relaxing muscles, deep breathing, and meditation are three ways to relax.

Chapter Review

Words to Know

Define each term below in your own words.

1. stressor _____

_____

2. meditation _____

_____

Relax!

Read each statement. If the statement is true, write **true** on the line provided. If the statement is false, write **false** on the line.

_____ **1.** Major life events, such as a parents' divorce, can cause stress.

_____ **2.** Being late is not a cause of stress.

_____ **3.** Stress causes your muscles to relax.

_____ **4.** Relaxing comes naturally. It cannot be learned.

_____ **5.** Breathing deeply can help you relax.

_____ **6.** Meditation is a way of emptying the mind.

_____ **7.** You should practice relaxing every day.

_____ **8.** Sighing is a way to relax.

Getting Personal

Can you think of any other ways to relax when under stress? Explain them below.

_____

_____

Chapter 3

Stress and Fitness

Chapter Objectives

- Explain how being physically fit can help reduce stress.
- Plan an exercise program.
- Identify ways to improve eating habits.

Words to Know

nutrient (NOO-tree-unt): any food or substance that the body needs to work properly

caffeine: substance found in foods, such as tea, coffee, and chocolate, that speeds up the body systems

stimulant: a type of drug that speeds up the nervous system

aerobic (er-OH-bik): exercise that raises the heart rate for a prolonged period of time

The Break Up

Lorena came home from school. She went straight to her bedroom and took a box of cookies from under the bed. Within an hour, she had eaten all of the cookies.

Lorena's sister came into the room. She looked at Lorena staring off into space. She noticed the empty cookie box.

"Lorena," she said. "You've got to stop this!"

"Stop what?" asked Lorena in a tired voice.

Her sister turned off the radio. "Ever since you and Ken broke up, you've been a blob. You are making yourself feel worse. No man is worth this!"

Tears sprang from Lorena's eyes. "I know. I feel terrible. But, what can I do?"

Lorena's sister threw a pair of jogging shoes at her. "Put these on," she said. Then she picked up the empty cookie box. "You've got to stay away from these."

Lorena knew her sister meant well. But, what good would it do to change her shoes?

What do you think Lorena's sister has in mind?

Fitness and Stress

Lorena is feeling stress from the break up with her boyfriend. She is depressed and lacks energy. When she shuts herself away and eats too many cookies, Lorena adds to her stress. Lorena's sister wants to help reduce Lorena's stress by helping her get physically fit.

Lorena's sister is right. Being fit means being healthy. Improving your health improves your ability to handle stress. Exercising regularly and eating a balanced diet improves your health and helps you stay fit.

Exercise is important in many ways. Through exercise, you can work off much of the extra energy that comes with stress. Certain types of exercise can also strengthen the heart. They help prevent stress-related health problems, such as heart attacks. Exercise also improves the way you look and feel about yourself. It reduces nervousness and depression.

Good eating habits are equally important in staying fit. Your body needs certain **nutrients** (NOO-tree-unts), or substances it needs to work properly. Without these nutrients, your body does not have the energy it needs to stay strong.

Experts think 50-80 percent of all illnesses are stress-related.

Some foods can actually cause stress. Foods such as tea, coffee, and chocolate contain **caffeine**, a substance that speeds up the body's systems. Caffeine is a type of **stimulant**, or drug that causes the systems of the body to speed up. The effects of caffeine do not last long. When the effects wear off, you may feel more tired than you did before. This is because your body is exhausted from working so fast!

Changing your exercise and eating habits can be a challenge. But it is worth the effort! This chapter will give you some tips on how to get started. Like learning to relax, take it one step at a time.

Circle the number that best describes your fitness habits. Be honest—you'll get more out of it!

1. I eat a wide variety of foods.

| 1 | 2 | 3 | 4 | 5 |
| Rarely | | Occasionally | | Usually |

2. I avoid sugar and caffeine.

| 1 | 2 | 3 | 4 | 5 |
| Rarely | | Occasionally | | Usually |

3. I exercise whenever I feel stress.

| 1 | 2 | 3 | 4 | 5 |
| Rarely | | Occasionally | | Usually |

4. I try to limit the amount of fatty foods I eat.

| 1 | 2 | 3 | 4 | 5 |
| Rarely | | Occasionally | | Usually |

5. I think fitness is important.

| 1 | 2 | 3 | 4 | 5 |
| Rarely | | Occasionally | | Usually |

Now take a look at what you circled.

- "4's" and "5's" are great. Give yourself a hand.
- "3's" mean you have some room for improvement.
- "2's" and "1's" are signs you could improve your fitness level.

Planning an Exercise Program

Lorena and her sister began their exercise program by walking around the neighborhood. After four weeks, they began to jog short distances. Even though Lorena didn't always feel like exercising, she kept with it.

One day, on her way out for a jog, Lorena noticed herself in the mirror. She really liked what she saw! She had lost a few pounds and looked better than she had in a long time. Lorena realized that her hard work had paid off. She felt better about herself and was better able to cope with stress.

Lorena discovered a few of the benefits of exercising regularly. Here are some steps to follow if you want to start your own exercise program:

Step 1: It is a good idea to speak with your doctor before starting an exercise program. Your doctor can give you guidance and suggestions regarding the type of exercise best suited for you.

Step 2: Choose an activity that appeals to you, one that you will stick with. There are many different ways to exercise. **Aerobic** (er-OH-bik) activities, or exercises that raise the heart rate for a prolonged period, are one type. Walking quickly, swimming, and bicycle riding are examples of aerobic activities. They help strengthen your heart. Other kinds of activities, such as weight lifting, will tone your body and keep it healthy. Team sports, such as soccer, are additional ways of exercising.

What kind of aerobic exercise do you enjoy?

Step 3: Set exercise goals. Start slowly. Add a little time or work harder each week. Gradually, get to the point where you are exercising for half an hour three times a week.

Step 4: After each exercise session, notice how your body feels. Congratulate yourself each time you finish working out. Don't quit if you miss a session. Just start over right away. Remember, changing habits takes time!

➤ No Excuses

It is easy to find an excuse for not exercising. Read the following situations. Suggest a way each person could stick with his or her exercise program.

1. Jenny started an exercise program to relieve her stress. She began by walking six blocks three times a week. She was doing great until the cold, snowy weather set in. "Oh, well," said Jenny. "I guess I'll have to wait until spring to exercise."

   _____

   _____

2. Joel decided to lift weights to get in shape. He bought some free weights and borrowed a book on weight training. For a while, he stayed on schedule. Then Joel began to skip his workouts. He decided they were too lonely and boring.

   _____

   _____

Eat Right to Feel Right

Eating right is another important part of staying fit. Your body needs a wide variety of foods to stay healthy. When you eat too much, or too little, you do not have the energy you need to cope with stress.

The following simple tips can put you on the road to better eating!

1. Use the food pyramid, found on the next page, to help you to plan a balanced diet. Most of the foods you eat should come from the bottom part of the pyramid. Eat fewer of the foods at the top.

2. Drink six to eight glasses of water each day. Water helps to clean out the waste in your body. It also helps to control your hunger and helps in weight loss.

3. Think about the reasons why you snack. Is there something other than hunger that causes you to eat between meals? If so, find another way to cope with your feelings. If you're angry, go exercise until you are feeling calm. If you're bored, call a friend and go for a walk. If you're tired, take a nap.

4. Say good-bye to alcohol, caffeine, and sugar. These things drain your body's energy. You'll find your body is stronger without them.

➤ **Think About It**

Other than hunger, what causes you to snack?

Better Eating

The Food Pyramid

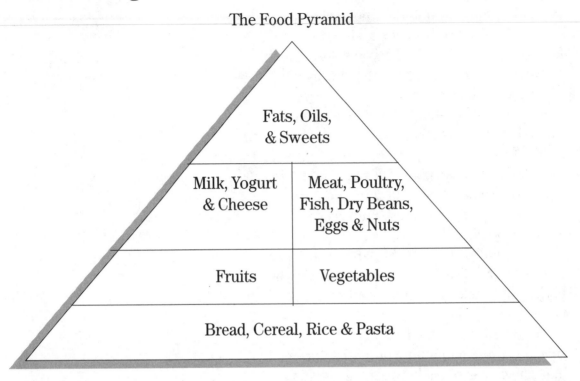

1. Use the food pyramid to write a daily menu. Include three meals and two
   snacks. Be sure your menu contains:

- 9 servings of bread, cereal, rice, and pasta (1 serving=1 slice of bread; 1 ounce
  cold cereal; 1/2 cup cooked pasta or rice)
- 3 servings of fruit (1 serving=1 medium piece of fruit; 1/2 cup of berries;
  3/4 cup fruit juice)
- 4 servings of vegetables (1 serving=1 potato or carrot; 1/2 cup cooked
  vegetables; 1 cup leafy vegetables)
- 3 servings of milk, yogurt, and cheese (1 serving=8 ounces milk or yogurt; 4
  ounces soft cheese; 2 ounces hard cheese)
- 2 servings of meat, poultry, fish, dry beans, eggs, and nuts (1 serving=3 ounces
  meat, fish, poultry; 1 cup beans or lentils)

2. Now follow your menu for one day. Describe how you felt during the day. How did your planned meals differ from the type of meal you usually eat? How did your snacks differ? _____

_____

_____

Help is Good!

Changing your exercise and eating habits can be a challenge. For this reason, it is a good idea to have help or support when beginning a fitness program. Here are four ways to get the help you need:

1. Invite members of your family to join your fitness program. Agree to keep only healthful foods in the house. Try cooking meals together. Go for walks with each other.

2. Work out with a partner. This will help you stick to a schedule and make the exercising more fun.

3. Become involved in school or community sports. Contact the local parks and recreation department, the YMCA, and your school for information about the kinds of programs available. Many of these organizations offer free, or low-cost, programs and equipment.

4. Forgive yourself if you miss your workout or eat something fatty or filled with sugar. Think about all the positive things you have done. Then, start over again with a smile!

If you work-out with a friend, you can both benefit.

Chapter Summary

- Good fitness means exercise and eating right. When your body is fit, it has more energy and is better able to fight stress.
- An exercise program involves seeing a doctor, and selecting an activity you enjoy. When planning your exercise program, set reasonable goals and start slowly. A workout partner can help keep you on the pathway to achieving your goals.
- Use the food pyramid as a guide to eating right. Drink six to eight glasses of water a day. Stay away from sugar, caffeine, and alcohol. If you snack when you're not hungry, explore your feelings. Find ways to feel good that don't involve eating.

Chapter Review

Words to Know

Complete each sentence with one of the words below.

aerobic   caffeine   nutrients   stimulant

1. Coffee and chocolate contain _____.

2. Caffeine is a type of _____.

3. Walking briskly is an _____ exercise.

4. Your body needs _____ to stay well.

About Fitness

1. Why do you think you should see a doctor before beginning an exercise program? _____

_____

2. Marcia decided to start exercising to get into shape. She began by running three miles. The next day, her whole body ached. What do you think Marcia did wrong?

_____

_____

Getting Personal

What are three things you intend to do this week that will help improve your fitness? _____

_____

Chapter 4

Think Less Stress

Chapter Objectives

- Describe the relationship between your thoughts and stress.
- Practice two ways to reduce stressful thoughts.
- List four ways to get help with stressful thoughts.

Word to Know

imagination (i-maj-uh-NAY-shun): the act or power of creating images or ideas

When You Worry Too Much

Andrew saw a sign in a store window. It read "Help Wanted. Part-Time Afternoons." Andrew really wanted the job, but he was too afraid and nervous to go in. "What if they think I'm stupid?" he said to himself.

Andrew asked his sister to go to the store and get an application for him. As soon as he began filling it out, his shoulders became tense. He felt cranky.

"I'll never get this job. I don't have any experience," he told his mother.

"You have experience doing work around this house," replied his mom.

"Right. I'll put that on the application, and they'll think I'm really dumb!" said Andrew.

Somehow Andrew managed to complete the application. He knew he should deliver it in person, but he mailed it instead. "It doesn't matter how the application gets there," he said to himself. "I'll never get the job."

That night, Andrew dreamt the store owner opened his letter and laughed like a monster. Then he ripped up the application and threw it away. Andrew woke up feeling sick.

What is causing Andrew's stress?

Your Thoughts and Stress

Andrew thinks poorly of himself. He worries all the time. He is convinced that he will fail. This makes him nervous, afraid, and cranky. His thoughts are causing him stress. They are actually making him sick.

Your thoughts are very powerful. They can help you succeed in life. Or, they can cause you to fail. The trick is to control your thoughts, instead of letting them control you.

The first step is to become aware of your thoughts, and the effect they have on you. Here are some typical thoughts that can cause stress:

Can you add to this list?

- "I'm not good enough."
- "I'll never get this done."
- "I'm really stupid."
- "Nobody will listen to me."
- "Nobody cares about me."
- "Everyone will laugh at me."

In this chapter, you will learn how to reduce stress-causing thoughts like these. You will discover how to replace them with positive thoughts such as:

- "I am good enough."
- "If I work hard, I'll get this done."
- "I'm smart enough to figure this out."

- "What I have to say is important."
- "I care about what happens to me."
- "I am proud of what I can do."

Changing your thoughts takes practice and work, just like relaxing, exercising, and eating right. Start now by closing your eyes. Say to yourself, "I can do this." Then, get to work!

➤ Stress Buster

Rewrite each story. Change each stressful thought into a positive one.

1. June really likes Harry. "He'll never notice me," she says to herself. "I'm too plain." Every time she's in Harry's company, June gets nervous.

   _____

   _____

   _____

2. Ben just struck out, making the last out of the game. His team lost. "I failed," says Ben to himself. "I'll never play baseball again." He goes home feeling like a failure. _____

   _____

   _____

3. Kim signs up to audition for a part in the school play. When the time comes, she panics. "If I get up there, everybody will laugh at me. I can't do it." Her right eye begins to twitch. _____

   _____

   _____

Seeing Yourself Succeed

The owner of the store sent Andrew a letter asking him to come in and interview for the job. When Andrew read the letter, he froze. What would he do? He would certainly make a fool of himself!

He went to his friend Jack. Jack seemed to always succeed whenever he tried new things. The few times that Jack wasn't successful didn't seem to bother him too much.

Andrew asked his friend for suggestions on how to handle the interview. "Here's what I do," responded Jack. "I use my **imagination** (i-maj-uh-NAY-shun), or the power to create an image or idea. I imagine the whole thing in my head. I see myself relaxed and in control. I think and do all of the right things. Then, when I am in the real situation, my imagined feelings take over."

Andrew eyed his friend suspiciously.

"It works," Jack said. "I'll show you how."

Jack had Andrew get comfortable on the couch. Andrew closed his eyes. He listened to Jack. Jack spoke to him in a quiet voice. Then he said:

Imagine yourself completely relaxed. Your shoulders are loose. You are breathing deeply. This is how you feel at the job interview. You see yourself neatly dressed. You look great! You feel confident. When you meet the store owner, you are still relaxed. You smile. You shake his hand. Your grip is warm and strong.

Jack is using a guided imagination exercise to help Andrew. Guided imagination exercises are an important way to reduce stress.

Using your imagination can help you relax.

Professional athletes use them to see themselves making all the right moves. Cancer patients use them as part of their treatment for getting well. Even people looking for jobs can use them to relax before interviews.

You can use your imagination to help you relax and prevent stress. In the following exercise, you will work through the steps in this process.

> ## Guided Imagination

1. Find a quiet place. If you like, put on slow, soft instrumental music. Close your eyes.

2. Take several deep breaths. As you exhale, see and feel the tension drain from your body.

3. Imagine you are relaxing in a favorite place. It should be a place where you feel safe, comfortable, and happy. Think about the sounds, smells, and colors of this place.

4. Focus on how your body feels in this place. Your shoulders, neck, and forehead should feel loose and relaxed. Your breathing is deep and even. You feel good about who you are.

5. Now imagine yourself at your big event. Your body feels just as relaxed as it felt at your favorite place. Your breathing is deep and even. You continue to feel good about who you are.

6. Continue to imagine yourself at the event. You do all the right things. Your thoughts are positive. You are confident. Your mind and body are relaxed.

7. Bring these thoughts and feelings with you as you open your eyes.

If you did this exercise, where was your favorite place? Describe this place using as much detail as you can.

_____

_____

Stopping Stressful Thoughts

Andrew practiced his guided imagination exercises. In spite of the exercises, he still kept thinking, "I'm not ready. I'm not ready!"

Andrew decided enough was enough. Each time he started to think "I'm not ready," he clapped his hands. "Stop!" he said to himself sharply. "I *am* ready!"

Andrew is using another important method of controlling his thoughts. Experts call it thought-stopping. Thought-stopping is used when you have recurring, or repeating, stressful thoughts. Here is how the process works:

Say "STOP" when stressful thoughts get in your way.

1. Identify the stressful thoughts that keep coming up again and again in your mind. (Remember, a stressful thought is one that keeps you so worried, scared, or upset that you can't act in a positive way.)

2. When you notice the thought, interrupt it right away. Do this with a loud noise, such as clapping. You can even say "STOP!" aloud.

3. Replace the stressful thought with a positive one.

Here is an example of thought-stopping in use:

Patty is baby-sitting. She keeps hearing noises in the kitchen. She checks the kitchen and finds it empty. Yet, she keeps thinking: "Someone is in the house." She knows it isn't true but she keeps getting more and more scared. Suddenly, she realizes what she is doing. "STOP!" she yells. "This house is safe. I checked the kitchen, and everything is fine!"

➤ Thought-Stopping

1. Rewrite the following three steps so they appear in the correct order.

   A. Interrupt the thought.

   B. Identify the thought.

   C. Replace the stressful thought with a positive thought.

   _____

   _____

   _____

2. Think of a time when a recurring thought caused you stress. What was the thought?

   _____

3. Suppose you had used thought stopping to control the stressful thought. Identify two positive thoughts you could have used to replace the stressful one.

   _____

   _____

Help is Good!

So far, this chapter has examined things you can do to control your thoughts. There might be times, however, when you cannot stop these thoughts by yourself. If you cannot control stressful thoughts or are thinking about hurting yourself or another, get help. *You are worth it.* If you feel that you need some assistance, you could:

1. Talk to your friends or family members. They may be able to give you ideas about how to handle the situation. If necessary, they will get you the extra help you need.

2. Sometimes, you can't talk to your friends or a family member. Share your thoughts with a teacher that you like and trust. Your school might even have a counseling center that can offer you support and advice.

3. Find a community counseling service. This type of facility is staffed by professionals who can help. Some specialize in the problems faced by teenagers. Most cities and counties have low-cost, or no cost, counseling services. They will be listed in the phone book under "Government."

4. Speak with your family doctor, or a minister, priest, or rabbi. They can direct you to further help.

The telephone book lists city and county resources.

HEALTH CARE AGENCIES
• AIDS Prevention and Information
• Family and Youth Services
• Family Violence Project
• Suicide Prevention Crisis Calls
• Teen Programming

1. A friend tells you she is really depressed. She can't stop thinking about taking her own life. Where might she get help?

_____

2. A friend tells you he thinks he might have AIDS. It is all he thinks about. Where might he get help?

_____

Chapter Summary

- Negative thoughts create stress. Positive thoughts can help you to prevent or reduce stress.
- Two ways to reduce stressful thoughts are guided imagination and thought stopping.
- Sometimes, you need help in stopping stressful thoughts. Friends, family, school professionals, and community agencies are possible resources.

Chapter Review

Word to Know

Use your own words to describe *imagination*.

_____

About Thoughts and Stress

Read the following thoughts. If the thought is positive, write **P** on the line. If the thought is negative, write **N**.

_____ **1.** "I can do it."

_____ **2.** "I'm no good."

_____ **3.** "Nobody likes me."

_____ **4.** "I'm too scared to do it."

_____ **5.** "I am worth it."

6. What are two ways you can use to control stressful thoughts?

_____

_____

7. List four places where you could get help in controlling stressful thoughts.

_____

_____

Getting Personal

What did you learn in this chapter that you plan to use during the next week?

_____

_____

Chapter 5

Time, Stress, and You

Chapter Objectives

- Explain the importance of using time wisely.
- Explore three steps to use time wisely.
- List four tips for using time wisely.

Words to Know

procrastinating (proh-KRAS-tuh-nayt-ing): to put
    things off, or to do them at the last minute
priorities (preye-OWR-uh-teez): important goals
productive: able to get the most done

Watching the World Go By

Mia came home from school. She threw her books on her bed and went into the living room. She sat on the couch and watched television for three straight hours.

When her mother came home, she was angry. "Mia," yelled her mother. "Why haven't you started dinner?"

Mia grumbled a response. She reluctantly helped her mother throw something together for the family's dinner. Then, Mia went back to watching television.

At 10 PM, her mother told her to go to bed. "I hope your homework is done," she told Mia. "Your English teacher told me you weren't doing too well in class."

Mia gulped. A paper was due tomorrow, and she hadn't even started it. There was no way she'd be able to get it done in time.

Mia felt terrible when she went to bed. She worried about what excuse she'd offer her English teacher. After tossing and turning half the night, Mia decided to blame the missing assignment on her home situation. She'd tell her teacher that her mother's working full time caused her too much stress. There just wasn't enough time to make dinner for the family and get her homework finished on time.

What is the real cause of Mia's stress?

Time and Stress

In Chapter 1, you learned that stress is caused by three things: your environment, your body, and your thoughts. What is the cause of Mia's stress?

It's coming from her environment. There are many demands on Mia's time. However, there are only 24 hours in a day. Since Mia is not using her time wisely, she is experiencing stress.

Handing in homework late can cause you stress.

Using time poorly is a major cause of stress. If you've ever put off doing a homework assignment until the last minute, you know this is true. Here are some signs of poor time use:

- Rushing at the last minute.
- Spending too many hours doing things that aren't important.
- Feeling like you never get anything done.
- Wishing you had more time to do things.
- **Procrastinating** (proh-KRAS-tuh-nayt-ing), or doing things at the last minute.
- Feeling badly about yourself.

> **Get Personal**

Which sign of poor time use have you experienced?

Reasons for Using Time Wisely

Using time wisely will help you to prevent and/or reduce daily stress. Using your time more wisely can help you to:

- Get things done that are important to you.
- Complete tasks on time.
- Have free time for fun activities.
- Feel more relaxed.
- Feel like you are in control of your life.

Record below how you've spent *most* of each hour during a 24-hour period.

Time	How You Spent **Most** of the Hour
Midnight–6 AM	
6 AM–7 AM	
7 AM–8 AM	
8 AM–9 AM	
9 AM–10 AM	
10 AM–11 AM	
11 AM–Noon	
Noon–1 PM	
1 PM–2 PM	
2 PM–3 PM	
3 PM–4 PM	
4 PM–5 PM	
5 PM–6 PM	
6 PM–7 PM	
7 PM–8 PM	
8 PM–9 PM	
9 PM–10 PM	
10 PM–11 PM	
11 PM–Midnight	

1. In blue, circle the hours that you spend meeting goals that are important to you. Are they mostly in the morning, afternoon, or evening?

   _____

2. In red, circle the hours that you spend wasting time. Are they mostly in the morning, afternoon, or evening?

   _____

3. What was the activity that wasted the greatest amount of your time?

   _____

Three More Steps to Better Time Use

Mia completed a time use log. She discovered that she was wasting too much time during her day watching television. She realized that her television habits were causing her stress.

Mia decided to examine her goals, or the things she wanted to achieve. At the top of her list was graduating from high school. Next was developing a good relationship with her mother. Mia decided that these were her top **priorities** (preye-OWR-uh-teez), or important goals.

The next thing Mia did was to break each goal into smaller steps. Every day, she set a certain amount of time aside for one or more of these smaller steps. She also was careful to include a slot of free time in her daily schedule.

What is your most important goal?

In planning how to use her time wisely, Mia followed these three steps:

Step 1: Set your goals. You have to decide how to use your time. If you are clear on your goals, you can make better choices about how to use your time.

Step 2: Put your goals in priority order. You may find that you have dozens of goals. If you spend equal amounts of time on each one, you'd get very little accomplished. That is why you need to set your priorities. Allow more time for goals that are more important to you. You may even decide that some goals should be eliminated from your schedule all together.

Here are some examples of both long- and short-term goals that may appear on your list:

- Graduate from high school.
- Go to college.
- Get a job.
- Learn to dance.
- Try out for a sports team.
- Get in shape.

Step 3: Break your goals into smaller steps. After you do this, plot the small steps on a calendar. Each day, cross off the steps that you have accomplished. You'll find that you get more done than you ever thought possible!

Too many goals can be unproductive.

➤ You and Your Goals

1. List four of your goals. _____

   _____

   _____

2. Arrange these goals in priority order. (**A** should be the most important goal.)

   A. _____

   B. _____

   C. _____

   D. _____

3. Develop a plan for achieving one of your goals.

   _____

   _____

   _____

4. Break one of your goals into five small steps. Write them on the lines below.

   _____

   _____

   _____

   _____

   _____

5. Make a daily schedule for yourself. Plot each of the steps you listed above on a calendar. Write in how much time will be needed for each step. Always include a little extra time for each step.

6. As you complete each small step, cross it off the calendar.

➤ **How Do You Feel**

After following your daily schedule for one week, answer these questions.

1. Were you able to stick to your schedule?_____

2. How did you feel when you were able to cross out a task on the calendar?

_____

3. Did you schedule enough time to complete each step?

_____

4. In making a schedule for achieving another goal, what would you do differently? Explain why._____

_____

_____

More Tips on Using Time

Mia found that using time wisely took practice. In the end, it paid off. She got her homework done. She got along better with her mother because she was able to get her work done. Because she was meeting her commitments, Mia was able to enjoy her favorite television show without feeling guilty. She liked reducing the stress in her life. Most of all, she enjoyed the feeling of being in control.

You can enjoy many of these same feelings by using your own time more wisely. Here are some more tips on how to do this:

- Review your time log to identify the time of day when you are most **productive**, or able to get the most done. If you are most productive in the morning, schedule your most important tasks at that time. If you are most productive in the evening, schedule the tasks then.
- Schedule a block of free time each day. You can use this time for fun, emergencies, or whatever you like.
- Limit the amount of television you watch. If you are like most people, you use it to relax or to be entertained. You can fill these same needs through exercising, reading, or being with friends.
- Get up an hour earlier. This is probably hard to do on school days. But, if you use the extra time for your most important goal, you may actually enjoy the time.

Chapter Summary

- Using time wisely prevents and/or reduces stress. It helps you achieve your goals and have fun.
- The first step in using time well is to identify your goals. Then, put them in priority order. Break the most important goals down into smaller steps. Plan when you will complete each step.
- Schedule your hardest or most important tasks for your most productive time of day. Leave yourself some free time every day. Limit the amount of television you watch. Add an hour to your day by getting up one hour earlier.

Chapter Review

Words to Know

Complete each sentence with a term listed below.

    priority   procrastinate   productive

1. She worked most in the morning. That was her most _____ time of day.

2. When you put things off, you _____ .

3. Use most of your time to accomplish the goal with top _____ .

Time, Stress, and You

If the statement is true, write **true** on the line. If the statement is false, write **false.**

_____ 1. You have no control over how you use your time.

_____ 2. Your top priority goals are the most important goals.

_____ 3. It is helpful to break your goals down into small steps.

_____ 4. A well-managed day does not allow for any free time.

_____ 5. Using time wisely relieves stress.

_____ 6. Rising an hour earlier will only give you additional stress.

Getting Personal

Was using the time log helpful to you? Why or why not?

_____

_____

Handling Stress

Words to Know

Match each word on the left to its meaning on the right. Write the correct letter in the space provided.

_____ 1. aerobic

_____ 2. caffeine

_____ 3. environment

_____ 4. exhaustion

_____ 5. imagination

_____ 6. meditation

_____ 7. nutrient

_____ 8. priorities

_____ 9. procrastinate

_____10. productive

_____11. stimulant

_____12. stress

_____13. stressor

a. event that causes stress

b. to put things off or do them at the last minute

c. deep, continued thought

d. exercise that raises the heart rate for a prolonged period

e. physical and social surroundings

f. a drug that speeds up the nervous system

g. important goals

h. body's reaction to a new or changing situation

i. substance the body needs to work properly

j. state of extreme tiredness

k. act or power of creating images or ideas

l. substance found in coffee, tea, and cola

m. able to get the most done

About Handling Stress

Answer each question in the space provided.

1. What are the three main sources of stress? _____

_____

2. Why is it important to learn how to relax?

_____

_____

3. Identify three ways to improve your eating habits.

_____

_____

_____

4. What are two ways to reduce stressful thoughts?

_____

_____

5. What are three steps in using time wisely?

_____

_____

_____

Getting Personal

What do you think is the most valuable thing you learned from this book? Explain why.

_____

_____

_____

_____

Glossary

aerobic (er-OH-bik): exercise that raises the heart rate for a prolonged period of time, 31

caffeine: substance found in foods such as tea, coffee, and chocolate that speeds up the body systems, 29

environment (in-VY-run-munt): physical and social surroundings, 6

exhaustion (ig-ZAWS-chun): state of extreme tiredness, 9

imagination (i-maj-uh-NAY-shun): the act or power of creating images or ideas, 42

meditation (med-uh-TAY-shun): deep, continued thought, 21

nutrient (NOO-tree-unt): any food or substance the body needs to work properly, 28

priorities (preye-OWR-uh-teez): important goals, 56

procrastinating (proh-KRAS-tuh-nayt-ing): to put things off or do them at the last minute, 52

productive: able to get the most done, 59

stimulant: a type of drug that speeds up the nervous system, 29

stress: the body's reaction to a new or changing situation, 6

stressor: event that causes stress, 16